How to overcome anxiety and panic attacks in 10 days

Re-educate your own body, without either medication or side effects, and stop being afraid

MAYA RUIBARBO

Ebook Disclaimer and Copyright

ISBN ***CDLAP00003224***

Table of Contents

CONCLUSION

Introduction

How I became a jibbering wreck in just 5 minutes

The story is not in the words; it's in the struggle.

Paul Auster

I felt elated on September 8th, 2013. For the first time after two months of hospitalization, surgery and convalescence, I was myself once again and believed to have regained control over my own life. I had taken the motorway leading to the western part of my region in order to stay at my grandparents' house for a while. There I hoped to recharge my batteries and enjoy long walks with my dogs out in the autumn sun, followed by pleasant conversations at dusk with my loving aunts and all the pleasures that country life brings to an urbanite. Thanks to the Cantabrian motorway's recent coming into service a few years ago, it should have taken me only a couple of hours of relaxed driving to reach my destination. I was about to leave behind the Central area of the region and and drive into Western Asturias, all the way down to the border with Galicia.

A joyful song of the 60's was playing.

And then it happened.

My hands started to shake.

First it was just a nagging feeling. A bluntness that bothered me in order to hold the steering wheel. But it got worse in a matter of seconds. Horrified, I noticed my upper extremities began to be paralyzed. I could not longer move my fingers, it was like wearing boxing gloves. I tried to hold onto the steering wheel with the back of my hand.

Then my feet and legs also stopped working, and became paralyzed too.

Meanwhile, my car went on running at full speed, more than 120 kilometers per hour (75 mph), and I noticed other cars passing me. They overtook me while unaware that at any time a catastrophe could occur. Because I could not longer drive my car. Neither could I stop it by operating the brake pedal with my feet, because my legs refused to obey my orders. And with my hands turned into stone, I was unable to reach the brakes. Besides, my arms pressed up against my body and glued there. I could not separate them.

The car was still going on its own.

Right there it began my odyssey. For the following two months nothing was left of the entrepreneurial, independent woman that I usually considered myself, a woman who had always made his own decisions. Instead it only remained a wreck.

But I found a way out. This is the account of my personal struggle and how I achieved that. I write it because I hope it can help many people who are going through the same or similar circumstances.

If this is your case, and this is why are you reading this introduction, welcome. The bad news is that if you suffer from anxiety attacks, also known as panic attacks, you will have to venture into the heart of darkness. The good news is that there is a way out, and it's just as rapid and direct as was your downfall.

First of all I must ask you to be patient with me while reading this book. Sometimes, maybe even most of the time, it might seem that you're not going anywhere, and that all we do is delight in misery. Believe me, that's not the case. I wrote it intentionally this way. To actually help you, you need to go through the same process as me and many others like me. Otherwise, when arrived at the definitive solution for your problem, you won't be able to fully apprehend it, let alone implement it in an effective manner, and finally, at last, free yourself.

Like a Little Thumb in the land of anxiety, we should be picking up bread crumbs one by one because at some point we got lost and now we need to find again our path back home. In this case our goal lies at the point at which you will be free of these horrific attacks forever. You should arrive there quickly. Without sequelae. No need for medicines. Just keeping yourself in action, equipped only with your personal courage and resilience, building inside you.

So to get the most out of this book and to achieve what you intend, that is, to get rid of all those panic attacks once and for all, I recommend you to read these pages in a sequential orden, and calmly. It will not take long. The text is short and easy to read. You just have to adapt it to your own personal needs. And afterwards proceed with action plan once you are ready.

My greatest reward should be to help you get rid of those terrors that plague your life. Even if you have managed so far to avoid them for a long time, you know as I do that Fear –yes, with a capital 'F'- is able to lie dormant for years, hampering, oppressing and taking away your freedom, weighing you down until the end of your days unless you do something. Do you wish to be a person permanently cursed? Of course not.

Please pay attention to this book during one or two afternoons. Let me lead you by the hand. Let's reach together the light at the end of the tunnel and defeat terror.

Our journey begins here.

Maya Ruibarbo

Chapter 1:

What's happening to me? Learn what you are facing

Choices are made in brief seconds and paid for in the time that remains.

.Paolo Giordano

I did not know what was up until days later. After saving myself miraculously on the freeway -soon I will tell you how I managed and how, in my case and from the beginning, it became clear one of the main characteristics of panic attacks: they don't kill-, I came into the emergency room of the Central Hospital, accompanied by my mother. I had to cancel definitely the long-awaited trip to the west of my region. My mind began to shape an emerging driving phobia or fear of driving, that would manifest itself profusely along the following weeks.

An internal medicine trainee thought that maybe I needed phosphorus (or perhaps was it potassium?), when I told him what had happened with my limbs. Clearly he had the best intentions when he prescribed vitamin supplements, but that being said, his recommendations just meant an even longer ordeal for me.

I'm not complaining. There are other people who suffer repeated panic attacks throughout their lives. Neither traditional nor alternative medicine provide an effective solution. Because there is none. It's that simple.

There is a solution within reach that you haven't noticed so far

Don´t worry. This solution actually exists. And it always works. It's YOU.

Now you must be thinking this is all nonsense, 'hooks' to sell this book with a cheap psychology of the market.

But you have to give it a try. I was the first one to doubt this method. But then it worked for me. And it will work for you too. It's just common sense in action.

Several weeks had passed by, and driving had become real torture. Previously, it gave me my greatest pleasure. But after being about to die, or so I thought, several times, not anymore. Frankly, because of those terrifying experiences, I now consider myself one of the world's leading experts in panic attacks.

I say this unashamedly, because my knowledge comes from hard experience. Experience is the best teacher, as the saying goes. I know what fear is, what panic is. I still remember the time when I realized that my whole body was slowly becoming paralyzed, as if I had suddenly become paraplegic, and the terror I felt. I barely had the time to get out of the driving lane in the center of the city, and move my vehicle the best that I could to a nearby lay-by reserved for buses. I next tried to open the car door because I was choking, but neither my hands, arms, legs or feet responded. Paralysis was gradually invading me. “What will happen when it reaches my head?”, I thought terrified.

And that was one of my good days. I am very stubborn, I always have been. And I strove to keep driving every single day. Although I had a mortal fear. Although the attacks had ceased to be limited to my fear of driving, and now produced anywhere indoors at any time. But I knew that if I gave up, if I stopped getting in my car out of panic, I would never be able to drive again. It had already happened to lots of other people. I would become disabled forever, because of my car always being an extension of myself, one of the most enjoyable places on earth in my point of view. My driving aimlessly along secondary bewitching roads and paths had allowed me knowing new fascinating places. I did not wish that part of my life to go down the drain.

I took several days for me to be diagnosed as suffering from panic and anxiety attacks. In the meantime, I had to be back in the ER. My mother drove me there with all the symptoms of a false heart attack. I started then, as I do whenever I have a problem, an intensive Internet research. Also it was at that point, and because of what happened at the ER, that I asked for an appointment with a social security psychiatrist.

Remedies on the market

What my Google search showed was disheartening.

• Partial solutions

•Psychotropic treatments, involving antidepressants and axiolytics

• Relaxation and meditation techniques

• Esoteric practices involving soul retrieval

Thanks to this exhausting and seemengly useless process, I was able to start connecting the dots. Also, the psychiatrist I visited soon afterwards, although she did not solve the problem, contributed her bit. She did not seem to give great importance to what was happening to me. I felt strangely relieved. She simply suggested that when one of those panic attacks began, I shoud breath into a paper or plastic bag. Thus I should be able to retain more carbon dioxide and improve the alkalosis caused by hyperventilation.

This was easier said than done. For starters, to grab the plastic bag in the midst of the attack was quite an impossible task for me. My paralyzed and stuck arms would not let me budge an inch. Instead, I tried to breathe into my purse, which I had previously placed open next to me, on the passenger seat of the car, by leaning my torso and chest forward. It did not work, either. Once or twice I forgot to keep my purse open by my side, so when the disorder erupted, I was not able to proceed. I just lay there, like a dismantled and useless penguin toy, crying my heart out, and brooding over life that, for some inexplicable reason, had decided to take my future away.

How to learn from Sherlock Holmes: Connect the dots

Prospects looked completely unfavorable for me. However, it's always darkest before the dawn. I began to recognize signs that the wind was changing, and started connecting the dots. The situation was about to take a turn for the better. I did not know then, but I'd just taken my first step back from the Heart of Darkness.

Chapter 2

I'm going to Die, right?

Falsehood is never in words; it is in things

Italo Calvino

Remember the motorway, when first my hands and feet got paralyzed? How did I manage to get away and emerge unscathed?

I looked for a nearby exit, that was less than three kilometers (around two miles) away. But because I was so scared, even a moment seemed like an eternity. To make matters even worse, that section of the motorway did not have a hard shoulder. Not that I could park on it, anyway, with my hands turned into stone fists, or so it seemed to me. There was no way I could shift to a lower gear. I kept my fists on the steering wheel to swerve when I took the next exit available. And there my car plunged, still at full speed, towards a roundabout. My proverbial luck made a Civil Guard patrol being right there, seemingly committed to the task of traffic surveillance.

“Great”, I thought, “for once I wish you guys would come and try to fine me, so perhaps you would be able to help me stopping this damned car”.

Between you and me, it was the first time in my whole life that I was glad to spot a Civil Guard Highway Patrol.

But it seems I am forever subject to Murphy’s law (you know, "anything that can go wrong, will go even worse than you’ve ever imagined"). So they did not notice my car’s zigzag course, the excessive speed at which I proceeded right into the roundabout and above all, my distorted face. No way. The agents found no signs of alarm and did not even look in my direction. Damn!

Using my fists instead of hands to handle the wheel, I took the old national road, and came to a halt at a restaurant parking lot not far away. It was full of trucks, but there was still plenty of room to maneuver. With my last ounce of strength, because my fists hurt like hell whenever I used to turn the wheel, I parked my car between two trucks. I did not even bother to put my car in neutral. I simply stopped the vehicle in spite of my swollen and insensitive foot. Finally I turned off the engine.

My parents had to to travel for an hour to come and pick me up. It was another ordeal. My hands kept inert and paralyzed. Luckily I managed to click with the side of my hand on their number, stored in the phone memory. Interestingly enough, when they arrived I felt better, more secure. I improved my general state of health within seconds. I even was able to drive again my car all the way back home, because my mother sat next to me throughout the journey. Panic attacks only started when I drove by myself.

Unconsciously, and because of my journalism skills, I began to gather some useful information. I recommend you to do the same before throwing your hat into the ring. This last reference comes from the 'trick' that I will explain to you a few pages further on, and that should serve you well, to get rid of panic attacks forever.

Let's recap:

□ What characterizes all panic attacks or anxiety? What do they all have in common, even if they manifest themselves in the most varied forms depending on the individual who suffers? FEAR. Pure fear, panic fear, terror. At first, we are afraid because we do not know what is happening to us. Afterwards, once we learn more about what has happened, the initial fear becomes FEAR TO FEAR itself. Fear of future panick attacks. We do not wish to go through something like that never again. Then the fear of possible repeated bouts of anxiety causes most of us to avoid situations or places that are thought to cause the attacks. In my case, I might have chosen never to drive again, since entering my car seemed to trigger attacks. Others opt to give up their jobs, since stress is too much for them; or even never again enter a lift/elevator because it was in one of those that he or she suffered the first panic attack.

Let me tell you about a girl I met briefly in a company for which I worked. I was hired specifically to replace her, and I was told her story. Then I happened to meet her when she was forced to come once again to her previous workplace, in order to sign the settlement which put an end to her labor relationships with the company. Obviously she left as soon as she could.

Those were the times previous to the world economic crisis. Back then, people still did not feel the urge to secure and retain their jobs by any means. But symptoms were there. The company accumulated many debts and it was only a matter of months that, due to the negative domino effect, she and many others workers were fired. Creditors were already to the phone to make claims. The manager of the company pushed relentlessly for the finance department to reconcile statements immediately so as to assure their account activity was correct. However, there was no possibility of reconciling accounts, at least not until the company customers had payed what they owed. If customers did not pay, there was no way this company could in turn pay suppliers. As simple as that.

But this girl I am telling you about felt responsible for what the company was going through. She was a diligent worker. She insisted on meeting the given guidelines. She formatted hundreds of Excel tables and charts, looking for ways to reduce costs and solve the imbalance between income and expenditure. Nothing worked, of course. And stress was building up as scolding from her boss went on and on. He was really angry at her for failing to meet some insane expectations. As time went by, tables and statistics and estimates piled haphazardly on her table.

The mess surrounded her every day she went to work, It got worse. Creditors became more and more insistent, and the phone kept ringing. By order of his boss, she had to lie and drag her feet, while looking for a way out of the labyrinth. Her nervous system endured a brutal overload for several months, she was on the edge of a nervous breakdown, and finally exploded.

It happened in the parking lot of the company, when she left home at night, after one of those marathon and crazed workdays. His body perfectly reproduced, down to the smallest detail, the symptoms and suffering of a heart attack. After being subjected to a thorough medical examination, despite having no physical ailment, she obtained medical leave immediately.

Soon afterwards, she quit his job. This young woman did not see herself able to return to the rack that her job had recently become. And above all, she never wanted to experience again another panic attack. That was her main motivation to leave.

The fear that is not such fear

Allow me to repeat something said before: the first time an anxiety attack occurs we feel a tremendous amount of fear. Fear is what's happening to us. But from then on, we fear or are afraid of fear itself. We already know, because we have been informed by the medical staff, that what happened to us was a panic attack. The initial terror of not knowing what was happening to our body is replaced by panic to relive the same circumstances. And chances are that it happens again at one time or the other. Once anxiety attacks start, the pattern is etched in the body, which will rewind it whenever it perceives the signals considered dangerous or threatening. As we shall see, our body is similar to a best friend who wants to help us at all costs, but in its eagerness to lend a hand, becomes a wiseass and gets us in trouble.

The foolproof method underlying Laws of Robotics

□ Better come off the motorway. The sooner the better And try not to kill anyone in the process. That was what I thought when I left the highway. I managed to do it, and nobody, not even myself, got hurt. By the way, I do not know if you've ever read the book *I, Robot*, by Isaac Asimov, or some other work of this author, but his three Laws of Robotics fit perfectly with what happens to us when we suffer panic attacks.

Let's remember first their original content:

1. A robot may not injure a human being or, through inaction, allows a human being to come to harm.

2. A robot must obey the orders given it by human beings, except where such orders would conflict with the First Law.

3. A robot must protect its own existence as long as such protection does not conflict with the First or Second Laws.

We will now replace "robot" by "your body" and "human being" by "yourself". *Et voilà!* As if by magic we've perfectly described a panic attack.

1. Your body will never hurt you or, through inaction, allows you to suffer damage.

2. Your body must obey the orders given by you, except where such orders would conflict with the First Law.

3. Your body must protect its own existence as long as such protection does not conflict with the First or Second Law.

Soon we will see how the body automatically processes the Three laws. In the next chapter, be surprised about the procedure.

Chapter 3

The Road to Hell is paved with good intentions

The trouble with a great sadness is that it doesn't fit inside your body.
Manuel Rivas

The saying used as this chapter's title could not be more true. And it may as well apply to our body. It is clear that our body wants the best for us. Always. Its survival depends on our continous support, through proper nourishment, providing water enough, moving around properly, and not stuffing it with junk food and harmful substances. And also, our body requires not to be excessively alarmed. This may sound like gibberish to you, but that's how panic attacks brew. My own case is a good example, for this to be better explained.

The surgeon who operated on me had the best intentions. After surgery, she wished for me to have the best possible recovery. A tract from my small intestine had been removed. The portion involved in the resection was rather long. We could call it a cut-and-paste surgery. After cutting off the damaged section, she had to put together the tract's two ends left in the body. Her biggest concern, once the procedure was completed, focused on reestablish the intestine's normal functioning as soon as possible.

Obviously, I came out of surgery in a semi-conscious state. But once I woke up, I felt a lot like moving around. My body wanted to go back to normal the sooner the better. I do not know how I did it, but I was able to sit up in bed just a few hours after surgery.

Apparently it's the way I am. Twenty years ago I had a similar operation, hospital staff wouldn't let me out of bed, fearing my digestive system would not take it so soon. But when I finally walked down the hallway, I.V. included, I went ahead, fast and light, becoming an object of admiration of all nurses that marvelled watching me pass by. After lying down for so long, I felt free. I just wanted to move around on my own. My body was shaking, because it felt so happy to be released from confinement. Medical personnel wisely let me have my own way, so I had about the fastest spontaneus recovery in history.

But 20 years later, it was a different story. In the beginning, I went through the same process. Right after surgery, it only took me a few days to start walking up and down the aisle as a runaway. I needed so much to move freely and to expend stored surplus energy. Lo and behold, I bumped it the surgeon who led the team that operated on me. She caught me red-handed and exposed. Logically, she looked horrified fearing that at any moment I could tear the stitches and all her work would have been in vain. Not to mention the whole shebang about my tummy's internal sutures being damaged, and causing a gastrointestinal (GI) perforation (hole). That would be the mother of all disasters. I could read what was going through my doctor's mind as if she was just saying it aloud.

Doctor Bogey-woman

At that point she would use the same method employed by moms who do not wish that their kids bite off more than they could chew. Moms conjure up the bogeyman for their little ones. And it works. Out of fear children will behave themselves. Right there, my doctor lectured me, her serious speech surpassing those of the greek Demosthenes. I was forbidden to further wander down the aisle, I should go to bed right away, and stay there. Every day I was allowed to sit down just for a while. I shouldn't walk by myself and –this was what struck me most- I should be prepared to face a long recovery ahead, and only God knew how long I still had to remain hospitalized.

Well, I payed attention to her ... sort of. I kept doing some of the stuff my body asked for. My particular Good Samaritan returned from time to time to lecture me again. Neither she nor I knew it then, but she was placing a program into my mind at the same primal level that the mind uses. That is, she was programming me thoroughly for what would come next. My body listened intently to every word, and absorbed the message as an earnest student.

Unfortunately, the message my body caught was:

"You can not care for yourself alone ... you can not manage things by yourself ... Inability to care for yourself ... you can not manage by yourself ..."

And next my body translated as follows:

"I have been seized without previous notice, been knocked unconscious, I have been torn, and choped as a suckling pig, and then they told me that I can not walk or run by myself. It was a doctor who has just told me, so she must be right. "

My conscious self did not follow any of all this soliloquy. I was apparently happy because, after 15 days of terror in the hospital, I was discharged and able to go back to my everyday strolls. The first days of convalescence were spent quietly at my parents' house. I had company, so I did not feel alone. There were no significant problems, except for certain bouts of weakness, normal under these circumstances, and little else. My convalescence was longer than expected, because the scar on my belly would take a while to heal.

After a month I decided to resume my own life routine. Alone. Independent. And I took the Cantabrian motorway westward, in search of a few days in the peace of the countryside. The rest is history, as you know. My jorney began, but never ended.

What happened on that highway that stopped me in my tracks? I have already told you the storyboard. But there is a parallel version of what was happening, and it consists in my body's reflections as I drove westward. For the first time after surgery, I was in my car, none of my family or friends nearby in order to help me out. The inner dialogue of my body might have been something like this: "Oh my God, she is by herself. And the doctor said she could not fend by herself. We're dead, because we are not ready yet to go on. The doctor said it would require a great deal of time before we could manage on our own, and it has only been a month since she said that. It's still too soon, too soon. We have to stop this whatever it takes, before a disaster occurs".

Do you understand now my body's reaction? To make it easier for you, nothing better than to describe it graphically on the next page. The first part shows the normal reaction of a healthy person (both physically and mentally), when required to take action. The second part lists the process that occurs when a body acts dysfunctional, because **it is afraid**.

Functional Body Behavior

Need to act for whatever reason that may arise

*

Emotion that precedes and accompanies action

*

Need for action

*

Apply energy

*

Decision

*

Action and movement

Dysfunctional body behavior

We have experienced some circumstances perceived as dangerous in the past. But now we must act again.

*

Fear and instinct of self-preservation appear

*

Need for action

*

Apply energy

*

Fear interferes. We become paralyzed

*

We can not complete action

*

We keep trying to act

*

Action - paralysis fight each other

*

Comes the panic attack and anxiety

Activating First Directive in order to survive

Do you remember Isaac Asimov's Laws of Robotics? When your body chooses a dysfunctional behaviour, it just turns on First Directive on its own. Oh my God, you're in trouble.

Let us never forget one thing: fear lies at the root of panic / anxiety attacks. Even if it manifests itself in very diverse ways. We shall see next.

Chapter 4

Damn, my body is launched. How do I stop it?

1. Your body will never hurt you or, through inaction, allow you to suffer damage.

2. Your body must obey the orders given by you, except where such orders would conflict with the First Law.

3. Your body must protect its own existence as long as such protection does not conflict with the First or Second Law.

After launching the First Directive, your body takes the initiative. Driven crazy by the urge to protect you at all costs, and scared to death at what has already happened once, and what might happen again, your body chooses the panic attack as a means to frighten you.

Yes, you read it right. The ultimate goal of panic attacks is to actually terrorize you, so you should be discouraged to atempt what body believes to be “crazy things”. So you wouldn’t dare to budge. Because if you dare, something bad could happen. So your body feels desperate to paralyze you and is trying to tell you: "You please stay very still, no more scares, once was enough." This First Directive drags along the Second and Third ones, and that’s when a panic attack is due… full steam ahead.

Learn how to deal with your Rebellious Inner Child

It's like you had a unruly inner little rebel in your hands. The more you insist on carrying on your life as normal, the more he or she strives to incapacitate you. He insists that “it’s for your sake, it’s all for your sake”. So little by little you start procrastinating or stop performing certain tasks or functions, for fear of recurrent panic attacks. At that point you find yourself chained to those attacks. For the rest of your life. And God forbid you persist in shaking off the chains. If so, panic attacks may worsen to assume alarming proportions. Not to mention the variety and extravagance shown in such seizures. If there was a Oscar Academy Award for Creativity related to panic attacks, your inner toddler could probably qualify for one.

To whole scenario is already depressing enough. But to cap it all, your body firmly believes that a panic attack is an effective protective strategy. Then a panic attack should be initiated at the slightest hint of a danger or a threat. What we've got here is a completely distorted perception. Take people suffering agoraphobia for example: they are often terrified by busy streets and open spaces for no reason. Because there are fears in all shapes and sizes, that your body assimilates and integrates due to one or more unpleasant past experiences.

Among these fears:

 Erotophobia: fear of sex

 Anuptafobia: to being left alone

 Nyctophobia: severe fear of the dark

 Hydrophobia: Fear of water

 Cronofobia: fear of the passing of time

 Hypochondria: worry about having a serious illness

 Acrophobia: fear of heights

 Enochlofobia: of being in a crowd

□ And so on and so forth. There are fears related to almost everything.

So there I was, with my body out of control and blocking me, trying to scare me to death day in and day out. Personally, I have nothing against the contemplative life, but it should be optional and not mandatory as my Inner Rebel intended to impose.

I have already said that the first hint to come out of the mess I was dwellling came from a psychiatrist of the National Health Service. She did not give much importance to what was happening. That paradoxically encouraged me. Although the doctor was reluctant, she ended up giving me the typical medication prescribed in these cases. Medication which, incidentally, is **useless**. I am positive about that, because I have suffered this terrifying experience, and so had other people around me. No traditional or alternative medicine has been shown to be very effective in treating panic attacks. Relaxation techniques do not serve any purpose either. Neither exercises to regain your lost soul.

KEY QUESTION:

□ THE ONLY SOLUTION TO THE PANIC ATTACKS IS UP TO YOU: People trying to help you at best may offer palliatives. But if you wish healing for real, remember that it was you (your body) the one who triggered the process. As a logical consequence, it is also you the one who will have to take appropriate action to re-educate your body, in order for it to stop behaving like a hysterical spoiled brat. All you have to do: cowboy up man (woman)! Once you get the ball rolling, immediately the rest of the way will immediately be easier.

□ In fact, when you get to end up the attacks, which take just a few days, you will be having fun... almost. Please don't get mad at me because of this last statement, I know you're really going through tough times. No wonder that to qualify a panic attack as 'fun' sounds quite a blasphemy to you. I would have thought the same during that horrible time when I suffered so much. Please try to believe this in advance, you will seen it confirmed soon. Once you have already begun, and are deeply involved, you would go on, because you'll have learned how to handle the previously terrifying panic attacks and now you will begin to appreciate the truth of the well-known dictum: "What doesn't kill you makes you stronger".

□Your body will be horrified, not knowing how to react to your strange behavior. It even might wonder if you have a masochistic streak, when you apply the sole remedy that stops panic attacks forever. (In the next chapter we will see a first example, about how my brother got rid of his anxiety issues).

Chapter 5

There is no turning back: move forward, then

We do not see things as they are, we see things as we are.
El Talmud

I promised you I was going to tell the story of how my brother managed by himself to overcome his panic attacks, and here it is. I did not even know about this, until my mother told me when I started having to deal with my own overwhelming experiences, that were about to bring me to the point of dispair. My brother's experience turned out to be the second milestone that helped me to get rid of my personal ordeal. There was a third one, consisting on a simple video on the Internet, and that was final and decisive.

The story of my brother starts, like many others, in this time of world economical crisis, that entails the need to seek work wherever opportunities arise. He had joined a multinational company in Madrid several years ago. He was rather satisfied with his working condistions, and was reasonably comfortable, although he missed his homeland. Finally he quit and moved closer to his (our) family. His previous company, which had once been public, granted workers a five-year grace period during which they were allowed to return if they regretted having left, provided that during that time span arose a suitable position for them.

By the time te economic global crisis erupted, my brother was back home, but his new job was less than perfect: it involved pluses and minuses. Among the disadvantages, a co-worker that seemed to have a lot of time to spare. He was truly a pain in the neck, and insisted on making my brother's life miserable. My brother ended up resigning.

Bad timing, right when the financial crisis reached its peak and unemployment rates skyrocketed. My brother's hope to find easily and quickly another job went down the toilet, along with many businesses that were forced into bankruptcy by the crisis.

Forced into a very difficult position, my brother began to consider returning to Madrid. He didn't get a kick out of going back to the stress of daily life and crowds in the city, but the truth is that he had been highly regarded in his previous post and their bosses and colleagues had liked him a lot. Once he hinted that he was thinking of going back to work, several of these colleagues pointed to a certain position that would soon become vacant and that, they said, would suit him perfectly.

Determined not to remain unemployed much longer, he grabbed the bags, rented a small apartment on the outskirts of the metropolis, as it was all that he could afford, and returned into the fold of large companies. He resigned himself to his fate of having to live away from home.

Paying attention to our interior monologue

His body, however, did not agree. It had heard the interior monologue that my brother's mind was carrying on and knew that despite all the apparent advantages, this arrangement was in truth not convincing at all. So, guess what? My brother's body decided to help him decide. To put it another way, to stack the deck in his favour. If my brother needed a little push to return "where the heart takes you", his body was ready to comply. And in a big way.

The first panic attack happened suddenly. Without further ado, a few days after he had returned to work, my brother began suffering from suffocation. He was choking and couldn't breathe at all, and even feared to be having a heart attack. He went to the doctor, who prescribed him well-known psychotropic substances such as benzodiazepines, and also anxiolytics. That is to say, lots of pills as usual.

You know it's no physical cause: the mental pathway

My brother listens flabbergasted after being examined by the staff physician: There's no physical cause for his ailment. He comes back home for a few days' rest after the attacks and brings all his pills along with him, just in case. He fears that his attacks prevent him from ever being able to work again. But afterwards he reflects that, if everything is mental, then taking his medication makes no sense. And bravely, he decides to cope with panic attacks on his own, without taking any drugs.

And he wins the batlle. After two or three attempts, he is free from panic attacks up to the present day. Pills remained sitting in a drawer. He never took them. He even fought successfully a panick attack during a flight taking him back to Madrid. The feeling that he was suffocating and soon would not have air to breathe and would be dead was overwhelming.

But that's the **KEY QUESTION**:

□ ***ALWAYS KEEP IN MIND THE FIRST DIRECTIVE: Our body on its own, never, never, never, never, ever, would hurt you. This is understandable, right? Because if it damages you it harms itself. Even disorders described as psychosomatic ones, such as panic attacks could be considered, are the human body's last resort to offer you a solution and to try to get you out of a point in your life when, for whatever reason, you have lost direction. Previously we said the road to Hell is paved with good intentions, remember? Well, you body is also full of good intentions. It can easily be way out of line when trying to "lend a hand".***

□ ***You could say that this above is plain common sense. And that you don't give a damm about robotic directives and other similar crap when you're having a panic attack. I totally, absolutely agree. If you find yourself paralyzed by fear, as it also happened to me, you only think about surviving the next minute. Fear of death is everywhere. But ...***

□ ***<u>But you have to take that step</u>. I don't know if you too watched the Indiana Jones films a long, long time ago. I did, and I loved them. In one of them,*** **Indiana Jones and the Last Crusade,** ***our hero was forced to take a leap of faith to save his father, who had been poisoned and could die in minutes. The leap of faith meant crossing over a Precipice where apparently there was no bridge. He had to walk into the void and advance, although he couldn't see any bridge under his feet to cross over to the other side. He risked instead a fall of many hundreds of meters, leading to certain death. Indy, of course, dared to take the first step over the cliff. Miraculously, he did not plunge. Something kept him suspended above the void! It turned out that, although he could not see it or touch it, there was indeed a bridge.***

□ ***In the next chapter I will tell you in detail how, in the wake of my brother's success, I also took my own leap of faith. And I will teach you the Do-It-Yourself (DIY) method related to panic attacks. A small step forward, and you will find the invisible bridge at your disposal, to help you getting rid of anxiety forever and be back to your old self again.***

Chapter 6

Three minutes gave me my life back

Don't believe everything you think.

Unknown

Day after day I climbed into my car and tried to reach my parents' house. A drive that should have been short –in the past it would take me less than 10 minutes- had turned into a daily nightmare that lasted two or three hours. I, with my insistence on pursuing the end of panic attacks, was not achieving any significant results. Attacks not only did not cease, but they got worse. I remember the day when I showed up in my parents' living room with a swollen puffy face and as if stung by singularly aggressive bees. I could barely speak coherently, because of Jaw paralysis. My mouth felt numb, as if having received a massive dose of lidocaine. I looked like a boxer being knocked out.

But this time I had ended up knocked out without having anybody else to blame. Unless, of course, we should consider my body as an independent being, since it had seized the initiative. In that case the truth is that my body was hammering me and winning this particular war between us. I insisted on going back to my normal life, my body inisted on "protecting me", because supposedly I was not able to manage by myself. That's what the doctor had said and it stood, so far.

Life or death situations

During the tug-of-war between my body and myself, I got to cope repeatedly with life-and-death situations. I will never forget another horrible afternoon when I left my parents' house to return to mine. I no longer felt strong enough to take the motorway surrounding the city, so instead I chose a route driving through the suburbs. It was a slower route, with lots of intersections and traffic lights, but in exchange it seemed to me safer. Why? Because if the panic attacks started again I could always pull over on the hard shoulder, or even to park in front of some garage's exit lane or access to a motorcycle parking area. Whatever I could find first during the emergency.

The attack indeed recommenced. But I think I mentioned earlier in a previous chapter that my body was always learning new ways to torture me. This time it did not wait until I could slow down and stop my car smoothly. in the middle of a neighborhood and walking speed. I had to go first , which had several lanes in each direction, and a huge roundabout.

Without warning (it wouldn't wish to alert me at no cost), my body suddenly triggered the attack. Next thing I knew, my hands were completely paralyzed. Not even could I take my hands off the steering wheel without feeling an excruciating pain. looked quickly to get out to a secondary road. I changed lanes while sweating and moaning. The next thing I remember, I was unable to turn so I missed the exit and I was quickly approaching a two-way road. In the exit lane on the right queued up several cars halted at a red light, and blissfully unaware of the disabled crazy woman driving her car too fast and out of control. My car was heading straight into them. Three seconds left ... two ... I got to see the look of horror on the nearest driver's face. When I was a few meters away from death -a frontal crash is the most common type of crash resulting in fatalities, even I would have been able to reduce speed- I miraculously regained the use of my hands. I could dodge the row of vehicles at the last second, and get into the right turn lane. A few meters ahead, I finally found a parking space.

This episode allowed me to recapitulate about what just had happened. The First Directive! The body wanted to scare me to death, but certainly was not actively seeking it out. When death risk came too close, basic survival instincts prevailed over the mechanisms of panic attack.

I began then an internal dialogue with my body. I was prone to take it easy, my body kept on the defensive. And for the first time since this unfortunate affair had started, I felt I had the initiative:

-Caught you! -I said.

-What ... do you mean? –I imagined my inner grumpy psyche replying so.

-You are not able to kill me! Well, you do know how to dodge and ditch when things get really serious! You just showed me! It's all turned out a bluff! - I felt I had this right to pick on my body a bit, after how it made my life a living hell during the previous weeks.

No answer. My body did not know what to say. So I continued:

-Well, from now on, I won't care what you do, or how difficult a time you are going to give. I've learned that you can not kill me, then I'm not afraid anymore.

In fact, I was still quite afraid, but terror had dropped a few degrees. When you know you're not going to end up dead in the adventure, because your body will find a way out, you feel safe again. Not entirely sure as before, but you've finally found something to cling to.

To say that this knowledge (no death ahead soon) healed me at once was far from the truth, but at least I knew I was on my way to improve. I went on several uneventful trips, driving around the commercial area next to my neighborhood. That zone did not bring back unpleasant memories. Neither dit it create fears and insecurity, as I was always driving near my appartment. Whereas the route to my parents' house remained an issue, and my dream of driving to the western wing of the region seemed destined to remain a pipe dream.

One afternoon I sat in front of my computer and googled, as many times before, the words "panic attack".

I remembered once again my brother's story, that as I said I had heard from my mother, since he was already back to his job in Madrid. I sighed and thought to myself that I would never be so brave.

But that afternoon another help came to me. From YouTube, to be precise. I carried out further research on anxiety attacks in my spare time. And finished every night very discouraged, because once and again I came to the conclusion that there was no effective panic attack's treatment or remedy. According to what I read and heard on the Internet, little progress had been made so far. Three weeks had passed while immersed in my very own nightmare, and I saw no clear signs of improvement on the horizon.

The best defense is a good offense

That video appeared just like any other, a video trying to sell something most people don't need.. But it lasted only three minutes, so I thought I had nothing to lose. "Let's see how long it takes to appear a link to a foolproof method's landing page", I bet against myself.

There was no link. The video lasted indeed only three minutes. It contained a single message: "Instead of running, face it." That is, instead of running away, face your anxiety problem head on.

I'll write this sentence again, because here lies the solution to panic attacks is. If I had to condense this book down to one sentence, it would be this one. In a minute I'll explain what I mean.

"Instead of running, do face your fear"

And again:

FACE YOUR FEAR

YET AGAIN:

FACE YOUR FEAR HEAD ON

At this point I can almost hear you cursing, and tearing me to shreds. "This author ... she has made me buy this totally useless book! What does she think I've been doing from the beginning, but facing my fear? She has taken me for a fool! ". When you have calmed down a bit, read on, because there is a knack. Yes, no catch. Not that you have not been doing well so far, actually your reactions have surely been the normal human ones since the world began.

THE TRICK IS RELATED TO THE MEANING OF THE VERB "TO FACE"

This keyword has a double significance.

Before I explain, we need to refresh our memories. Historical memories. Even prehistoric ones, if you ask me. Surely many of you already know what I am about to tell you next, but it will provide proper context for explaining better how to “face up to” fear and anxiety.

Throughout the ages... since Man and human ancestors in the evolutionary scale walked the planet, they faced a multitude of dangers. We all agree here, right? It was not exactly living in paradise on Earth. In fact, Earth was strewn with dangers for our forebears, much more dangers, difficulties, setbacks and problems than those that we now suffer in any civilized country. When primitive man came out of his cave, he could never be sure if he would live to see another day.

There was a lot of exotic wildlife. Man would be a tasty morsel for predators. There were floods, ice storms, landslides... whatever. That was no life. If you've ever watched a video of a deer in the forest - better if you have spotted one live, like it happened to me, but that is more difficult these days- you will have some idea of poor Homo sapiens high level of stress. A fawn is in a perpetual state of nervousness, looking around continuosly, always on guard because the next attack could happen anytime, anywhere. And when my two little dogs in high excitement actually chased the young stag, it disappeared in a heartbeat, faster than the speed of light. This cute animal was never ever able to relax.

Same happened to primitive men. They had to withstand all that stress, yoga classes still several million years away. So Human Body did bite the bullet and set out to find solutions in a hurry, because the case was urgent. Human Body found indeed three alternatives, and made them available to Human Brain. From then on, it was up to Brain to choose the option that best suits each situation.

Available responses are these, the 3 F's:

- Escape (Flight)

- Attack (Fight)
- Paralysis (Freeze)

Having to face an enemy which was superior in numbers and/or strength and organization, primitive man would take it on the lam, and end of story.

Same happened with animals. After all, why not admit that yes, our nature is derived from the nature of animals. Fight or flight, these two were the original instinctive reactions. But there was a third option, when the other two failed. Some species even chose this third way as the preferred one to react to a threat or attack.

This third way out of danger is Paralysis. By the way, I remember now an unfortunate day. I had started helping out in an animal shelter. For a rookie mistake of mine, I opened two little dogs' cages. These dogs never got along and should never be out together, as had strongly emphasized the lady in charge. But being almost an expert in How to Screw Up my First Days in a New Job, this time was no exception, you know?

I understood immediately why the strong warning about these two dogs. One second they were quiet, the next second one of them was snarling and chomping on the other with the worst intentions. It seemed ready to destroy its partner. I tried to separate them, but without success. Other shelter workers came when they heard me crying, there came the companions of the animal shelter, they used a hose to separate the murderous dog and its victim. By then the dog's body object of the attack, seeing itself in mortal danger, had gone completely rigid. All the blood was gone from his limbs and at first I feared we had arrived too late, and that the other dog would have finished the little one off. What I saw before me actually had all the appearance of a corpse.

I had a hard time. But while the animal shelter workers locked the perpetrator in an animal cage, resurrection took place. The apparently dead dog came back to life in two shakes of a lamb's tail. Amazingly it escaped unhurt, just a few scratches, but otherwise, it jumped up and down all happy.

This dog had successfully played dead, and thanks to this 'ploy' of Nature, it had survived the threat by instinctively freezing. Many other animals use the same technique. They get paralyzed or play dead when noticing the predator or threat approaching, hoping that in this way the attacker loses interest and passes by. Paralysis might be considered a very original variation of the flight response. But in this case we try to disappear by keeping ourselves immobiles, stuck in the same place. Sometimes it works.

These three responses, handed down from generation to generation, have served the human race until recently. But then modern times came: on the plus side, beastly physical aggressions greatly decreased, on the minus, it turns out that we now have some outdated reactions that now serve no purpose.

Many times I have wished to punch and bite my boss (or my bosses, almost all of them). A sharp bite and some kicks, I often thought, and I would feel good about myself again, by liberating my body's stored energy. However, luckily, mind is nearly always able to intervene in time. "You cannot do that, don't, control yourself, calm yourself, relax". So stress goes on accumulating. Nor could one trigger the Flight reaction. For instance, what would your colleagues say if you left your workplace every time a massive bummer arises? Nothing less than you had lost your marbles, I bet. This conduct would not be tolerated.

At present, these responses remain at an early stage when a perceived attack takes place. Reactions of fight or flight are no longer so directly implemented as before. Instead of biting or kicking the boss or colleague that bothers and angers us, we respond incensed and start an argument, for instance. Or when a friend hurts us, we might seek to avoid seeing him or her in the future. Also, if we have relationship issues – lack of assertiveness, as they call it now- we can choose to take refuge in vices like drinking, gambling and smoking. Through these vices we get to control and mitigate the impulses of the primitive brain and the limbic system, so that we are able to feel better. It also helps to minimize and reduce stress and release tension when one watches a football, soccer or basketball game on TV, for example.

What to do when the body feels overwhelmed

But what happens when stress levels skyrocket under exceptional circumstances? Remember the events that triggered my panic attacks? The surgery I had to undergo, followed by an equally stressful recovery period. My body considered itself to be a victim of an aggression, and also felt unable to defend itself, on account of its poor health and low energy at that time. It could not run away from the operating table, and afterwards, it suffered a long period of being trapped in a hospital bed. Neither could it attack doctors and nurses, because the brain would control and stop any violent impulses. My body could not even do a little exercise to speed recovery and expel some accumulated stress and tension, because my surgeon had exercise expressly forbidden.

Third valid reaction: paralysis

What options remained open, then? The third reaction, paralysis. My body resorted to that method the first time that I felt helpless, that is, the first time I was driving by myself after surgery and leaving the security of home behind. All my alarms went off. And the panic attack began. Later, having succeeded this first time, my body repeated the same pattern increasingly often, as my level of fear increased with each new attack.

Panic attacks feed off themselves. That means that each new anxiety or panic attack produces more and more fear. What's the worst that you can do when a panic attack takes place? To fight it head on.

"Pardon me?", you would say now, quite rightly. "Aren't you contradicting yourself about what you recently commented on the YouTube video? You insisted that the trick was precisely to cope"

Yes, and no. Because there are different ways and means to cope with such an attack, as you will learn in Chapter 7. For now, we are here:

> *In order to know your enemy, you must become your enemy.* . Carlos Ruiz Zafon

Of course your body is not your enemy, but the quote is still valid. The vast majority of us understandably offer intense resistance when we start suffering panic attacks. There is an urge to flee from the scene, as we strive for the attack to be over the sooner, the better, so we can feel well again.

Paradoxically this turns out to be the worst path you can choose. What you have now, if you suffer or have ever suffered anxiety attacks, is that your troops are out of control, retreating is disarray because of panic. The more you resist and oppose the current situation, the more you will feed back attacks.

It's time to regroup under a single command. You will find how in Chapter 7.

Chapter 7

Go through this tunnel

Are we there yet?
Any seven-year-old kid

So far, we have seen how a front defense against a panic attack, by trying various tactics and remedies, all this defense does is to feed the attack.

We also know that the resulting anxiety and fear are the tactics of our body to keep us from living a situation considered highly dangerous and potentially harmful to us.

That is, fighting is no good. The flight, either. And we are our worst enemies.

Okay, are you willing to give up? No way. On the contrary, it is now when we are closer to the solution. Because, as Arthur Conan Doyle's immortal character Sherlock Holmes said, "once you eliminate the impossible, whatever remains, no matter how improbable, must be the truth".

So what do we have left?

TO SUFFER THOROUGHLY, THROUGH AND THROUGH, OUR PANIC ATTACK

In other words:

IF YOU CAN NOT STOP A PANIC ATTACK, SPEED IT UP

□ TURN THE ATTACK FULL UP

□ LET IT REACH MAXIMUM INTENSITY

□ ENCOURAGE IT, LET THE PANIC ATTACK TAKE OVER AND GO AS FAR AS POSSIBLE

At this point in the book, I bet you are about to think that it is I who urgently needs to get my head checked.

Whoa, whoa, not so fast, buddy! I'll explain it to you in depth right now. From here we go step by step:

1. **Panic attack begins** with all its signs and symptoms, a wide variety of them, which in my case meant paralyzed limbs and then gradually other body parts. You might be short of breath for starters, and right afterwards break out in a cold sweat, or feel lightheaded or sick to your stomack. Or you might come to believe that you are having a heart attack and you are going to die in minutes.

2. During previous panic attacks, your natural reaction was to try frantically to stop them, halting attacks in their tracks. DO NOT DO IT, FOR THIS ATTACK IS NOT REAL. IT IS NOT TRUE. You need to back off and detach from what your body is feeling and doing NOW. <u>Begin to see the panic attack before</u>

you, as if you were an spectator outside it. And mentally communicate with your body –aka your inner being- all the time, at a steady pace. You might use for instance these or similar sentences: "I know this is not real, it's a fabrication of yours to protect me. But it is not real, it is not true. I know you will not kill me or harm me in any way. It's not real, it's a lie. " And now let the panic attack reach its peak without offering any resistance.

3. Notice how your body produces all kinds of special effects to terrify and paralyze you, so as to fill you with a Stephen King type of terror. Only that this time you'll be watching from the outside. You feel it, but you're not that involved. Just like at the movies. It's similar to watching a horror film in the cinema. It might mean a terrible time for you for a while, but deep inside you also know for sure that the movie takes place entirely on the screen. However awful it may seem, it cannot reach you. It can neither affect you nor harm you. When the film is over, you drive happily home. Yeah, just like that, leaving fears behind you.

4. Your mind should relax while going through a panic attack. Just pay attention and watch the movie your body has just made up. For instance, I am rather bold once I catch the hang of things, So when getting rid of my panic attacks, I went even further and got cocky with my body, "Wow, how witty you are, pal. Now trembling, and what next? Uh, and now comes choking. I'm choking, I can't breathe. Ha, but I know for sure you are not suffocating me in the end. My goodness, I'm frightened to death. You sure can scare

the bejeezus out of me, right?" Indeed, I was having an extremely hard time, because first I drove my body mad. Then my inner self cranked it up more and more. Just let me tell you that running out of air is no small feat.

5. That's when you have to pull out all the stops, and do not be intimidated or impressed, no matter what your body does. If for instance you are running out of air, that's okay: tell yourself a hundred times there's no danger whatsoever of you choking. The good news is things get better soon if you stick to your guns and let your body get flooded with powerful panic attack symptoms, without them apparently affecting you. Remember to perceive all from an outsider's point of view. Within a short time, your body will eventually get tired and bored and **will stop the panic attack**. You've just succeeded in breaking the cycle. Forever and ever. Congratulations, you're free.

6. In my case, I remember that the panic attack reached unseen heights. I ran out of air, choking me, I thought I was going to die. But I said to my body: "It's not real, I know you, I know you and you will not kill me under no circumstances". Panic attack continued making a big display, and I tried to downplay its symptoms: "Let's see what you come up with next, by now I already know all about your old tricks. What about messing with my head for a change? You need to innovate, buddy, otherwise I will get bored". After two or three minutes, curiously, distracting thoughts started to invade my mind. For instance, I wondered if I had applied the parking brake when I noticed the

attack was about to start and stopped the car. Or what should I be eating for lunch. My brain's rambling distracted me. And the terrifying panic attack dissolve on its own into good humour.

Try it. What do you have to lose? If you've read this far, you've tried everything else and nothing worked. This technique has been used successfully by several friends, my brother, and myself. One of these friends, helped by an intelligent doctor, tried something similar. He was given a sugar pill (basically a candy) as a placebo, because he bit his tongue during seizures. Candy enabled a greater flow of saliva, and thus he tricked his brain. This friend has been seven years free of panic attacks, it's being two years since my last attack, and three years since my brother had one.

Best of all is that you will know, with abolute certainty, that panic attacks will never return. And that if they ever come back, by using the method described above you will be able to ignore them and go on with your life as usual.

How to put an end to your body's nasty magic tricks

That's why panic attacks are over. Your brain and your body both know that their free ride has come to an end. You have discovered the secrets behind their unfortunate magic tricks. But, as far as you are concerned, there will be no encores!

It's entirely up to you. It is true that the solution is tough, especially when you first put it into practice. But think about having a very stressful and upsetting time for a little while whereas you fully master this technique. And you will never be scared again.

It is like going through a long tunnel of terror in an amusement park. There is light at the end of the tunnel; that's your destination. As you go through emerging witches and monsters, and cobwebs fall on your face and hands trying to grab and terrorize you. But it is not real, and at the end of the ride you leave the exhibition, and share a hearty laugh with your friends about how scared you were while it lasted.

LOOK OUT! BEWARE!

□ You will probably have one or two aftershocks of the original panick attack if you apply this technique (although there are people who have freed themselves of anxiety and fear by implementing it just once). But you'll never suffer a panic attack as intense as the original one. Subsequent aftershocks might occur twice or three times, always diminishing in intensity, and finally disappearing altogether.

□ It may happen that the first time you put this system into practice you may not be able to find the light at the end of the tunnel. At least that's what you got to think. But there is nothing to worry about. If you have taken medication in a hurry, because you though you wouldn't able to endure a panick attack without it, or if you have employed any other system that you often use when you suffer a panic attack, that's okay. You can always defuse the situation by talking to the body immediately after the panic attack begins. Because panic feeds on drama. Tell yourself, tell to your own body: "It's okay, you've made such a big scene. But you are my body, so you cannot hurt me or kill me EVER. I know that for sure. So no matter what you make up in order to scare me, I DO NOT BELIEVE IT'S TRUE. "

□ Because **you know with absolute certainty that you're safe**. Never forget this: YOU ARE ALWAYS SAFE. Once panic attacks are diagnosed, and dismissed the remaining possible causes, you will be fully convinced everything happening to you is mental, a misguided defense mechanism. You can then relax and enjoy the show. At last.

□ In fact, when my panic attacks had been reduced in two weeks to mere numbness of the fingers when driving, I came to enjoy the ongoing performance. I would park my car on one side of the road, smoke a cigarette -I still smoked at that time - and enjoy myself: "What will happen now? Will my feet start to tingle, perhaps? Oops, my hand gets no longer paralyzed? This body of mine is incredible, look what it was able to do! " And again, soon I would be distracted and unable to focus attention on the subject any longer. Thanks to my wandering mind, my poor body had no other choice but to call off the exhibition. THE END.

Use this simple technique and get rid of panic attacks FOREVER. Forever and ever. Go through the tunnel and be free. Of course, circumstances vary greatly from one person to another, but still panic attacks' background is the same for everyone. Because fear is a common emotion to all human beings, and so are the devastating consequences it carries when it gets out of hand.

Adapt and personalize this method according to your own particular circumstances, and fly free again. This method has worked for me and many other people, it should work for you too. That's why I wrote this book. Hopefully you will be soon able to join our community of people who have succeeded in getting rid of panic attacks.

> *"The greatest scourge of modern life is to give importance to things that do not really have it" - Rabindranath Tagore.*

Conclusion

Thanks again for download my book!

If this book was of any help for you, I would appreciate it so much if you:

Lend it: This e-book is lending enabled, so please, share it with a friend.

Recommend it: Please help other readers find this book by recommending it to friends, readers' groups and discussion boards.

Review it: Please tell other readers why you liked this book by reviewing it at one of the following websites: Amazon or Goodreads.

Thank you very much for taking the time to read it. I am at your disposal at:

- My Amazon author page
- My Goodreads author page

Maya Ruibarbo

Printed in Great Britain
by Amazon.co.uk, Ltd.,
Marston Gate.